The Lazy Pe Guide to Hap

by Ernie J. Zelinski

Cover design by Totino Busby

Send all inquiries to:
Thomas More Publishing
200 East Bethany Drive
Allen, Texas 75002-3804

To order additional copies:
Telephone: 877-275-4725 / 972-390-6300

Fax: 800-688-8356 / 972-390-6560

Visit us at: **www.thomasmore.com**

Customer Service E-mail: **cservice@rcl-enterprises.com**

Printed in the United States of America

Library of Congress Control Number: 2001092035

ISBN 0–88347-475-1

1 2 3 4 5   05 04 03 02 01

Introduction

Having written six books, I am always being asked by friends and acquaintances, "What are you writing now?" My next book was supposed to be a parable, a project which I have now set aside four times. My reason for advancing this book is that I have the sense there is a real need for it.

Perhaps it is no coincidence that you have encountered *The Lazy Person's Guide to Happiness*. There may be something in here that you need to discover, or be reminded about, in order to get your life back on track to contentment and peace of mind.

Because my best-known book is *The Joy of Not Working*, some people will think that the "lazy person" in the title of this book refers to me, the author. It does partly, since I am somewhat a lazy person, and comfortable with it.

However, the "lazy person" in the title also refers to the reader, who may need guidance or reminders on happiness, but doesn't want to read a time-consuming tome.

Clearly, happiness takes work, but it doesn't take a lot of hard work, as most people in Western society believe. Above all, happiness entails paying attention to life.

In the modern world, it's so easy to forget all the important things that contribute to happiness, and instead, pursue those that don't. For this reason, we should all have a small handbook to review from time to time.

Whatever you make of the collection as a whole, I think at least a few of my reminders will help you lead a fuller, more relaxed, and happier life.

Ernie J. Zelinski

Whether or not you are conscious of it, you are the source of all your happiness.

You have two choices:

You can read this book; or

You can refrain from reading it.

Either way, you can still be happy.

L ife is a game.

Happy people are the players.

Unhappy people are the spectators.

Which would you like to be?

Much of tomorrow's happiness will depend upon how happy you are today.

The question is, what seeds of happiness do you intend to plant before the end of the day?

To create more time for enjoying that mysterious and unpredictable phenomenon called life, minimize your search for the secret to it.

Wiser people than you and I have tried without much success.

Besides, you don't need to fully understand life to fully enjoy it.

Be clear that happiness doesn't care how you get there.

Indeed, not only does happiness not care how you get there; it doesn't even care if you get there at all.

Predict unhappiness in your life and you will become a psychic with a pretty good track record.

Happiness, it seems, doesn't like people who are desperate for it.

The desperate pursuit of happiness is one of the chief causes of unhappiness.

So, stop trying so hard to be happy, and let the good times roll.

In order to experience more happiness in your world, sometimes you must go backward before you go forward.

Don't ask why.

Some things just work better in practice than they do in theory.

To be successful at this game called life, often it takes not working so hard at it.

Take the time to drop in and think about what you really want.

The answers may surprise you.

> *"Unhappiness is not knowing what we want and killing ourselves to get it."*
> *—Don Herold*

Some important purpose to pursue;

Someone to love;
Something to appreciate today;
Something to look forward to tomorrow.
These bring much happiness.

What more do you want?

Just as important as deciding what you want in life is deciding what you don't want.

Allow yourself to give up those things that don't make you happy.

Oddly enough, they aren't always the easiest things to give up.

Accept that if you have been looking for happiness and haven't found it, you have been looking in the wrong places.

Don't allow advertisers or other people to dictate what you want in life.

As the graffiti writer declared, "You can never get enough of what you really don't need."

Understand that a want is not a need.

All your needs are satisfied today.

And they have been since birth.

Otherwise you wouldn't be alive right now.

You can do without most wants for at least a week or two.

Go without a want long enough and it will likely go away.

Desperately wanting things leads to most unhappiness in this world.

When you want something badly, work at giving up your desire for it.

Not wanting something is as good as having it.

And a lot less trouble.

S eriously consider what a blessing it is not to receive everything you pray for.

According to Saint Teresa of Avila, "More tears are shed over answered prayers than unanswered ones."

"We, ignorant of ourselves, beg often our own harms, which wise powers deny us for our own good."
—William Shakespeare

It's best not to waste time and energy attempting to blame others for your unhappiness.

No one should be able to affect the quality of your life.

And guess what?

No one does!

Except for you, that is, with your own thoughts and behavior in response to what others do.

The mark of your unhappiness is the depth of your belief in how much you are a victim of your circumstances.

Argue for why you are a victim, and guess what?

You are one.

You get to be right about it.

The question is:
Do you want to be a victim or do you want to be happy?

When you are looking for someone to blame for your unhappiness, you don't have to look far.

As they say in the Southern states, the biggest troublemaker in your life is the person in the mirror who every morning puts makeup on your face or shaves it.

"Most of the sorrows of the earth humans cause for themselves."
—Buddha

It may be difficult to find happiness within ourselves; but it is virtually impossible to find it elsewhere.

Given that most happiness emanates from the mind and soul, where do you intend to go in pursuit of it?

You may decide to go traveling in search of happiness.

"The further, the better," you think.

Surprise!

The only happiness you get to experience on Himalaya mountaintops is what you bring with you.

If you're in a hurry to find happiness, slow down.

Give it a chance to catch up with you.

"If you are not happy here and now, you never will be."
—Taisen Deshimaru

Keep in mind that life lived in anticipation of tomorrow, or regretting yesterday, is always a day short of happiness.

"No longer forward nor behind
I look in hope or fear;
But, grateful, take the good I find,
The best of now and here."
—John Greenleaf Whittier

Try going with the flow of life a little more.

Let things happen naturally instead of always trying to make things happen.

It's always easier to ride a horse in the direction it's going.

Before you climb over the fence to where the grass appears greener, try watering your side first!

B e the source of happiness instead of looking for it.

You won't have to look for happiness if that is where you are coming from.

> *"And be content with such things*
> *as ye have."*
> *—The Bible, Hebrews*

Have you ever considered that your envy is the happiness and enjoyment that you perceive everyone else is having?

Well, you should.

Perhaps people you envy are much more miserable than you are.

> *"I look at what I have not and think myself unhappy; others look at what I have and think me happy."*
> —Joseph Roux

To be happy is to have few wants.

To have fewer wants, count your blessings more often.

"Glad that I live am I;
That the sky is blue;
Glad for the country lanes,
And the fall of dew."
—Lizette W. Reese

A happy life isn't the absence of unhappiness.

Unhappiness will sneak into your life whether you want it or not.

So will happiness.

What you choose to do with either is up to you.

S tart living life according to the way things are instead of the way they should be.

Much unhappiness is caused by the belief that life should be different from what it actually is.

Accepting reality for what it is will liberate you from the imprisonment of what ought to be.

As Lenny Bruce said, "What is is, and what ought to be is a damn lie."

Hell is other people," declared Jean-Paul Sartre.

In the same vein, a friend says, "Human beings, what a stupid concept!"

The fact is, people are only human.

To be sure, if they weren't, life would be different.

Since people will continue to be human, it's best to accept them for what they are.

Adjust your behavior around them in ways that bring you the most happiness.

Hang around happy people.

Avoid unhappy people.

Fall in love with a happy person.

Marry that happy person.

A void falling in love with four
members of the opposite sex
at the same time.

D on't even consider marrying
someone with more problems
than you.

H ang around with people who wear
Mickey Mouse watches.

And be suspicious of those who wear
Cartiers.

You are responsible for your own happiness above any other.

The best way to avoid happiness is to become responsible for someone else's ahead of your own.

If you are a happy person, don't spend your time trying to make an unhappy person happy.

Near as I can tell, you have to be a magician to pull it off.

Don't waste time offering other people advice.

You will either lose or break even.

If the advice turns out bad, the person will be angry at you.

If the advice is good, the person will forget that you gave it to them.

It doesn't cost much to be kind, but it can be very costly being too kind.

The more you give to certain people, the more they will push their luck.

As Harvey Mackay wrote, "If you want to be a Santa Claus, your sled better be able to pull a trailer."

Don't spend your time on earth judging people.

It's tedious and won't make you happy.

Besides, this is God's job.

When someone or something puzzles you, SMILE!

M isery doesn't only love company.

It demands it.

For this reason, don't walk away from negative people.

RUN!

> *"Avoid the company of deluded people when you can."*
> *—Buddha*

It takes energy and precious time to argue with an unreasonable person.

Ask yourself what the payoff is.

And accept that there is insanity on both sides of the argument when you argue with an idiot.

Don't waste your time trying to convince some person that what he is about to do will get him into trouble.

The best way to prove a fool wrong is to let him have his way.

Be careful with your heroes. Don't put them on pedestals, because no one deserves to be there.

Don't waste time justifying yourself to your critics.

As an unknown wise person stated, "Any fool can criticize and most do."

Being liked by everyone is impossible.

Thus, seek the respect of others, not popularity.

Stick to being yourself and not anyone else.

When Leonardo da Vinci was asked what his greatest accomplishment in his life was, he replied, "Leonardo da Vinci."

In this regard, Zen masters don't ask us to be something or someone we aren't.

Instead, they ask us to be more truly and more fully who we are.

To paraphrase Mark Twain, if someone hasn't given you a compliment by the noon hour, then give yourself one.

Occasionally, you will be given the chance to be either intellectual or pleasant.

Leave being intellectual to others.

Waiting can be hard work and downright dejecting.

Instead of waiting for the phone to ring, phone someone else!

Be good to others, but don't expect a lot of gratitude in this world.

Remember that good deeds are seldom remembered and bad deeds are seldom forgotten.

Hang around wise people.

Listen to them carefully.

You will learn a lot about happiness
in a short period of time.

Someday you may think about
doing something that a wise
person says you will regret.

Be clear that you will regret it.

Stop complaining about everything imaginable to your friends.

After a while, you will sound like a poetry reading gone bad—even to yourself.

Getting upset over someone's rudeness drains you of power.

Besides, if someone is rude to you, there is a good chance that you have earned it.

You are in control over the hurt other people inflict upon you.

How much you are wronged is dependent on how much care and energy you put into remembering it.

Avoid potentially nasty people and dangerous situations.

In case you haven't noticed, it is always easier to avoid trouble than to get out of trouble.

The next time someone says something nasty to you, agree with them.

This way, there won't be an argument.

And you will leave the person perplexed at the same time.

If you end up getting into a fight, make sure that you win by at least half a mile.

A Scottish proverb warns us, "Friends are lost by calling often and calling seldom."

Remember that it takes ten times as much time and energy to make a new friend as it does to keep an old one.

> "Forsake not an old friend; for the new is not comparable to him: a new friend is as new wine; when it is old, thou shalt drink it with pleasure."
> —Apocrypha. Ecclesiasticus 9:10

Go slow when choosing new friends.

Quality beats out quantity ten times
out of ten.

Never lend money to a friend—
old or new.

In the event you don't get paid back,
you will end up losing both.

Whenever you refuse to forgive someone, you haven't imprisoned the other person.

You have imprisoned yourself instead.

So, be forgiving of others.

And even more forgiving of yourself.

Contrary to popular belief, revenge is not sweet and it won't bring happiness.

As the French proverb states, "The best revenge is to live well."

Do what is right even when what others are doing is wrong.

Clearly, even though a million people do a stupid thing, it still remains a stupid thing.

Stand above the crowd—even if you have to stand alone.

There is no greater way to gain self-respect and the respect of others in this world.

D epending on others to make you happy is probably the most difficult way to attain happiness.

Try lighting your own fire instead of waiting around to be warmed by someone else's.

"Happiness is not something ready-made Buddha can give you. It comes from your own actions."
—The Dalai Lama

Never wish deprivation or unhappiness on others.

What you would like to deny others, you will eventually deny yourself.

Your thoughts won't affect others; however, the thoughts will negatively affect what you attain in your life.

Therefore, grant to others the things and happiness you would like for yourself.

B elieve it or not. This is it.

This is as good as life is going to get right now.

The experience you have of it will be determined by your prejudice alone.

You may hope for, but you won't be happy with, an entirely easy life.

When you always do the easy and comfortable, life turns out difficult.

However, when you do the difficult and uncomfortable, life turns out easy.

Think about this carefully, and you will see that it applies to all areas of your life.

A lways do the right and honest thing, regardless of how difficult it may appear to be.

In the long term, it will be the easier and more rewarding thing to have done.

As Buddha says, "Karma means you don't get away with anything."

Your suffering is something you choose.

Experience it fully.

Without it you will not achieve personal growth and higher consciousness.

Think your problems are special and unique?

Well, there's only about ten major problems in life.

And everyone has variations of all ten.

So what makes yours so special?

The severity of your problems is a matter of perspective.

Change your perspective and most of them become insignificant.

Some of them will no longer exist as problems, but opportunities instead.

An old Chinese proverb states, "My house burnt down, but now I can see the moon."

Provided you look for it, there is a silver lining in every cloud, regardless of how dark it is.

However, you will fail to see the silver lining if you are expecting something worse—or much better.

Life is much easier when you take responsibility.

Taking responsibility is your willingness to be the author of all your experiences—including those that you are embarrassed about and don't make you proud.

Think about the consequences of your actions before you take them—instead of afterward.

This will do wonders for reducing the number of problems you have in your life.

"Don't buy expensive socks if you can never find them."
—Unknown Wise Person

Problems without solutions are something you dream up.

Ask around about your problems and people will give you many good solutions.

> *"When life's problems seem*
> *overwhelming, look around and see what*
> *other people are coping with. You may*
> *consider yourself fortunate."*
> *—Ann Landers*

An unknown wise person advises us: "The only way to prevent what's past is to put a halt to it before it happens."

If this sounds impossible, it is.

Since you didn't prevent the past from happening, there's no point sweating over it.

An hour of worry—whether about the past or the future—robs you of an hour of happiness.

Never cry over a glass of spilt milk. It could have been a bottle of Dom Perignon.

> *"Do not worry; eat three square meals a day; say your prayers; be courteous to your creditors; keep your digestion good; exercise; go slow and easy. Maybe there are other things your special case requires to make you happy; but my friend, these I reckon will give you a good lift."*
> *—Abraham Lincoln*

Understand that nothing is as serious as it first appears.

Today's crisis makes tomorrow's interesting story.

"There ain't no cloud so thick that the sun ain't shinin' on t'other side."
—Rattlesnake, an 1870s mountain man

Most circumstances are neither good nor bad, but our thinking makes them so.

So why not look at life as an adventure instead of a burden?

"Life is easier to take than you think; all that is necessary is to accept the impossible, do without the indispensable, and bear the intolerable."
—Kathleen Norris

Opportunity for happiness knocks often.

The question is, how often are you home?

"When one door of happiness closes, another opens;
But often we look so long at the closed door, that we do not see the one which has been opened for us."
—Helen Keller

A simple life is a happy life.

Life is simple.

But you make it complex.

Go back to the basics.

And see how happy life can be.

Making the simple complex
doesn't take ingenuity.

Making the complex simple, now,
that's ingenuity!

As the old saying goes:

"Keep doing what you're doing and you'll keep getting what you're getting."

So if it's working, keep doing it.

And if it's not working, stop doing it.

Simple how life is, isn't it?

Do something every day to make your life less complicated.

Learn to identify the unimportant.

You will find that life's a breeze when you work as hard at simplifying it as you now do at complicating it.

Suffering from boredom?

Try getting to the source.
Be clear that there is only one source.

> *"Something is boring me;*
> *I think it is me."*
> *—Dylan Thomas*

Some of the most fascinating things in this world are things which we don't go looking for.

Thus, allow more chance into your life.

The more chance you allow, the more interesting your world will become.

To conquer boredom, put your boredom at risk.

Too much safety is dangerous.

You can climb Mount Everest "because it's there."

Or you can climb an imaginary mountain "because it isn't there."

Which do you think will bring you more satisfaction and happiness?

Fame, fortune, romance, or adventure. Whatever your dreams, work toward them.

You will never get satisfaction and happiness from the things you intended to do.

Don't wait for retirement to be happy and really start living.

Invariably, people who try this find out that they have waited much too long.

As Henry David Thoreau warned us, "Oh, God, to reach the point of death and realize you have never lived at all."

The foundation for all happiness lies in health.

Physical, mental, or spiritual health—use it or lose it!

It is important to enjoy what *is* before it *isn't*.

We don't appreciate how precious something is until we lose it.

Often we don't get it back.

"Health is the greatest gift.
Our body is precious.
It is our vehicle for awakening.
Treat it with care."
—Buddha

"If you don't take care of your body,
where do you expect to live?"
—Graffiti Writer

You may have accepted the adage:
"Time is money."

Yet this adage is false.

Otherwise, we should also say:
"Money is time."

The fact is:

Time is worth much more than money.

Spend it wisely.

A void driving your car as if your journey is the only one on earth that is going to save the universe.

Stop and think about it,

And you will realize that your journey is rather insignificant in the higher order of things.

> *"The hurrier we go,*
> *the behinder we get."*
> *—Old Dutch proverb*

I f you must hurry, then hurry slowly.

Speed kills—in more ways than one.

"But at my back I always hear
Time's winged chariot hurrying near;
And yonder all before us lie
Deserts of vast eternity."
—Andrew Marvell

When you think that you don't have time to watch a beautiful sunset, think again.

The time when you most need to watch a sunset is when you don't have time for it.

> *"What is this life if, full of care,*
> *We have no time to stand and stare?"*
> *—W. H. Davies*

Pay attention to good advice which comes unexpectedly.

For example, the menu at a restaurant in my home town advises:

"If you're not served in 5 minutes, you'll be served in 8 or 9 . . . maybe 12 minutes. RELAX!"

To put more time in your life,
don't rush.

Slow down instead.

In a magical way, the world will
ease up for you.

No enchanting moment lasts forever. Therefore, savor it while it is still there.

"Seize the day and put the least possible trust in tomorrow."
—Horace

L earn how to live and be happy one day at a time;

And you will have mastered how to live happily ever after.

"Happy the man, and happy he alone,
He who can call today his own;
He who, secure within, can say,
Tomorrow, do thy worst, for I have
lived today."
—John Dryden

Celebrate the small things in life. They usually turn out much bigger than you could ever imagine.

Keep in mind that you can't truly appreciate the big things until you can fully appreciate the small ones.

And here is another reason to celebrate the small things:

There are so many of them compared to the big ones.

Everyone seems to want to be somewhere they aren't.

Choose to be where you are right now and you will be happier than 90 percent of humankind.

What is success?

And what is happiness?

Think about these a little today, and a little more tomorrow, and still more the day after.

See how your answers change with time.

If you expect to have it all, you will have nothing.

Learn to be happy with nothing.

And you will have it all.

"I have the greatest of riches:
That of not desiring them."
—Eleonora Duse

Remember that success invariably comes with a price.

Know what the price is before you seek it.

Being unprepared will mean you have to pay the biggest part of the price after your success—not before.

Most people will agree at some level that money doesn't buy happiness, but deep down they haven't accepted it.

Regardless of how old you are, you will show wisdom well beyond your years when you truly accept that money can't buy contentment and peace of mind.

> *"Mere wealth can't bring us happiness;*
> *Mere wealth can't make us glad;*
> *But we'll always take a chance, I guess,*
> *At being rich, and sad."*
> *—C.C. Colton*

Why waste so much time, energy, and money trying to buy the biggest house that your credit rating will allow?

Truth be known, a small house can hold as much happiness as a large one.

Sometimes it will hold even more.

"I suppose I passed it a hundred times,
But I always stop for a minute.
And look at the house, the tragic house,
The house with nobody in it."
—Joyce Kilmer

"Home is any four walls that enclose
the right person."
—Helen Rowland

Call forth the best you can muster for living life to the fullest regardless of how limited your funds.

As the Greeks say, "When you are poor, it is important to have a good time."

Take the time to drink quality wine or champagne at least once a week.

This is especially important when you have something to celebrate;

And even more important when you don't.

Zen masters tell us that we become imprisoned by what we are most attached to:
Cars;
Houses;
Money;
Friends and lovers;
Egos and identities.

Let go of your attachment to these things and you will be set free.

Since you will spend a third or more of your waking hours at your job, it is important that you enjoy it.

Happiness from our work comes only when it's of great benefit to ourselves and others.

So don't work just for the money.

You are a slave if you do.

Your work should enrich your mind and soul as much as your financial well-being.

"Get happiness out of your work or you may never know what happiness is."
—Elbert Hubbard

"If you have to support yourself, you had bloody well better find some way that is going to be interesting."
—Katharine Hepburn

You work best at what you most need to become.

So work to grow, not just to acquire.

Whatever you want to be, don't bother with other things.

For it's not what you become, but what you don't become, that will hurt most in the end.

It is all too easy to demand of life more than it has to give.

Try to be everywhere at once and you will get nowhere.

Try to do everything and you will do nothing.

Try to be loved by everyone and you will be loved by no one.

So follow your dreams; but know your limitations.

Avoid the extreme behaviors of indulgence and deprivation.

Make it a rule to practice moderation in everything you undertake.

Except, of course, for moderation itself.

Clearly, hard work doesn't guarantee happiness.

If hard work guaranteed happiness, over 90 percent of Americans would be happy.

Surprisingly, psychologists and psychiatrists say that only about 20 percent of the total population is happy.

The most difficult way to make a living is to work hard for it.

Hard work is the best thing ever invented for killing time—as well as you.

The secret is, work as hard as you have to for a comfortable living;

And as little as you can get away with.

You can't be happy if you are working too hard.

Just ask your friends and family whether they think you are.

Pay attention to what they have to say.

Answer this important question:

How many people do you know who on their death beds stated, "I wish I would have worked more"?

Always strive to create an excellent work-life balance.

Try to err on the side of leisure.

> *"If a man has important work, and*
> *enough leisure and income to enable him*
> *to do it properly, he is in possession of*
> *as much happiness as is good for any of*
> *the children of Adam."*
> *—Richard Henry Tawney*

Why not practice being a lazy but intelligent and highly productive person, instead of a hardworking but hardheaded and moderately productive one?

In other words, work smart and not hard.

> *"It is in vain that you rise up early and go late to rest, eating the bread of anxious toil for he gives to his beloved sleep."*
> *—Psalm 127:2*

Whenever you are doing something difficult or time-consuming, ask yourself what would happen if you didn't do it.

In the event the answer is nothing, or next to nothing, stop doing it.

Warning:
Be a bit lazy, but still be creative, active, and productive.

It is folly to strive for total comfort.

Comfort is a double-edged sword.

A little will increase health and happiness.

Too much, and it will destroy both.

Think about this quietly and carefully:

Years from now, as you review your life, what may you regret not having done?

Clearly, it won't be to have worked longer and harder.

And it won't be to have accumulated more possessions.

Whatever it is, shouldn't you be doing it now?

Within each of us, more than we ever care to admit, lies the power to change our lives.

We can have better health, deeper friendships, everlasting love, more riches, enjoyable work, and greater freedom.

The power lies not in getting to Heaven, but in using our creativity on earth.

> *"If your daily life seems poor, do not blame it; blame yourself, tell yourself that you are not poet enough to call forth its riches."*
> *—Rainer Maria Rilke*

The degree of your contentment depends on the quality of your thinking.

Your thinking can either make you miserable or it can make you happy.

The amount of time and energy required for each mental state is about the same.

Stop being so reasonable all the time. Go with your intuition a little more.

Some of life's best decisions are the ones least thought out with reason.

Of three precious resources in life—time, money, and creativity—the only one unlimited is your creativity.

Make creativity your number one resource, and time and money won't be as precious.

L ife's big changes—bad or good—
often come unexpectedly.

Be prepared for either.

Use your creativity to make the best of
the way things turn out;

And most things will turn out just fine.

Your thoughts may be:

"Easy words for you to say."

"Life is much more difficult than this."

No doubt life is tough.

However, you must ask yourself:

"Next to what?"

D on't allow your confusion about life to get you down.

An unknown wise person advised us:

"The fact is, you will leave this earth as confused as when you arrived.

"However, you will be confused on a much higher intellectual level and about more esoteric things."

You must be able to feel pain.

Otherwise, you can't feel joy.

So when it's time to laugh, laugh.

When it's time to work, work.

When it's time to love, love.

And when it's time to cry, cry.

Only then will you be fulfilled.

Understand that happiness doesn't care how hard you work;

Nor does it care whether you wear designer clothes;

Nor does it care how fancy your car is;

Nor does it care if you get any of the other possessions you want;

And it clearly doesn't care how beautiful, talented, or intelligent you are.

There can be little happiness where wisdom is lacking.

Wisdom can't be purchased with money; nevertheless, there is a price to be paid.

Never refrain from paying the price, whether the payment is in time, patience, experience, energy, or perseverance.

Indeed, when you have to pay a lot for wisdom, you are getting a bargain.

Open your mind to opinions other than your own.

The people whose opinions you most fear may be the wise ones from whom you can learn most.

Happiness can only be experienced in the event life brings you what you are willing to accept.

Accept more of what life brings your way and you won't be insulted by reality.

Perhaps you have recently discovered reality and concluded that life isn't fair.

It isn't.

You have an obligation to do your best anyway.

Don't expect to find more happiness by changing your circumstances or your environment.

Just because everything is different doesn't mean anything has changed.

As they say in Zen Buddhism, "Wherever you go, there you are."

Many people are trying to be somebody they aren't.

Don't be one of them.

You already are somebody;

You are you.

And only by being yourself can you be happy.

Unless you make peace with who you are, you will never be truly content.

Self-esteem is something that only you can give to yourself, not others.

It is important to love yourself—even more than your mother does—no matter what others say or think about you.

So always live as if you like yourself.

Indeed, after a while, you won't be able to tell the difference.

Not only enjoy solitude; seek it.

Love yourself while getting to know yourself better.

Within yourself is the paradise you have been looking for.

Here you will find all the happiness you will ever need.

Don't be dismayed when the world hasn't brought you what you want.

For everything you have been denied, the world has brought you something better.

It is your duty to discover what it is.

Ten times as many good things happen to you as bad things.

Thus, it is your duty to spend ten times as much time ranting and raving about the wonder of life as you do complaining about it.

"Just think how happy you would be if you lost everything you have right now, and then got it back."
—Unknown Wise Person

Try turning every adversity into an opportunity with some benefit to you.

This way, adversity will have done half the work for you.

"If your house is on fire,
warm yourself by it."
—Spanish proverb

L ess is more.

Think carefully about how this applies
to most areas of your life.

"Be content with what you have;
rejoice in the way things are.
When you realize there is nothing lacking,
the whole world belongs to you."
—Tao Te Ching

You have the power to limit your happiness with presumptuous hope more than you can ever imagine.

It's best to eliminate all desire for things beyond your reach.

Keep in mind that happy people care not for what they can't have.

To admire without desire is their secret.

Try living by this motto:

"Happy to have;

"But just as happy not to have.

"And happy to be;

"But just as happy not to be."

There is no better way to experience freedom and peace of mind.

To fully enjoy anything you are doing, do it as if it were your last act.

Buddha tells us:

"As you walk and eat and travel, be where you are.

"Otherwise you will miss most of your life."

Whether or not it is clear to you, the world is as perfect as it can get.

It is what it is.

And this is all that it needs to be for you to love it and be of service to it.

*"It is so.
It cannot be otherwise."
—Inscription in a cathedral in Amsterdam*

Your seriousness can get in the way of having a good time.

Oscar Wilde wisely observed, "Life is much too important to be taken seriously."

And don't even think about trying to refute him.

Consider each day you haven't laughed, played, and celebrated your life to be a wasted day.

To experience much love is to experience much happiness.

In your universe, if love is scarce, who is not creating it?

Clearly, you are ultimately the source of all the love in your life.

As the Beatles sang in one of their songs:

"In the end, the love you take is equal to the love you make."

According to a Hindu proverb, "True happiness consists in making others happy."

As far as possible without surrender, be a kind, gentle, generous, and loving person.

Share whatever happiness you experience with others.

In this way you will multiply the happiness that comes into your life.

You were given three special gifts
when you were born:

The gifts of life, love, and laughter.

Learn to share these gifts with the rest
of the world.

And the rest of the world will play
happily with you.

When happiness forgets about you, see what treasures you can find in your unhappiness.

It won't be long before happiness remembers who you are, and sneaks back into your life again.

Some days you may doubt your happiness.

Don't!

Think too much;

And you will think yourself out of it.

Prescription for Lifelong Happiness

Purpose enough for satisfaction;

Work enough for sustenance;

Sanity enough to know when to play and rest;

Wealth enough for basic needs;

Affection enough to like many and love a few;

Self-respect enough to love yourself;

Charity enough to give to others in need;

Courage enough to face difficulties;
Creativity enough to solve problems;
Humor enough to laugh at will;
Hope enough to expect an interesting tomorrow;
Gratitude enough to appreciate what you have;
Health enough to enjoy life for all its worth.

If you want to live a long and happy life, forget how old you are.

This is more important the older you get.

Again, clarify what things matter most to you.

Ensure that they aren't sacrificed for the things that matter least.

There's nothing wrong with working diligently for money and the many good things money can buy.

However, ensure that in the pursuit of money, you haven't lost the priceless elements of happiness that money can't buy.

Priceless Things That Money Can't Buy

Physical health

Self-reliance

Quality friends

Satisfaction

Respect of others

Reputation

Good character

Playful attitude

Longevity

Personal creativity

Achievement

Loving family

Integrity

Peace of mind

Sense of humor

Street smarts

More Priceless Things That Money Can't Buy

Patience	Gratitude
Compassion	Empathy
Mental health	Ability to handle money
Warmth	Generosity
Humility	Greatness
Charm	Physical Fitness
Self-esteem	Time
Spiritual fulfillment	Wisdom

Never lose sight of your true wealth, the ability to think, creatively and spiritually.

It is better to have a million dollars of thinking ability than a million dollars.

The million dollars can be lost easily.

Your million dollars of creativity and spirituality is always there whenever you need it.

If you believe that happiness can be bought, then why don't you try selling some of yours?

Always keep in mind that happiness is a mode of traveling and not the destination.

Zen masters tell us that we corrupt the beauty of living by making happiness the goal.

They say happiness is the practice of living in the moment;

It's in everything we do.

Rule #1: Be happy with who you are, where you are, and with what you have.

Rule #2: When you find yourself unhappy with what life brings your way, go back to Rule #1.

A lways be true to yourself.

Do not blindly believe what brings happiness, even what is said in this book.

Find out for yourself what brings joy and contentment to your world.

Your inner voice will tell you what will bring you peace of mind.

Listen to it carefully.

You will be able to tell when you have attained true happiness.

Real happiness doesn't cost much.

Unworkable substitutes do.

"To be without some of the things you want is an indispensable part of happiness."
—Bertrand Russell

A bove all, you don't have to do anything difficult to bring happiness into your life at this time.

Just choose it and it's yours.

Enjoy today as if it were your last day—because it just may be.

With this in mind, don't spend your time searching for the happy moment.

You are that moment.